Trace

Trace

poems

Brenda Cárdenas

 Red Hen Press | *Pasadena, CA*

Trace

Book design by Mark E. Cull. Layout assistance by Cid Galicia.
Cover art by Roberto Harrison

Library of Congress Cataloging-in-Publication Data

Names: Cárdenas, Brenda, author.
Title: Trace: poems / Brenda Cárdenas.
Description: First Edition. | Pasadena, CA: Red Hen Press, [2023]
Identifiers: LCCN 2022044714 (print) | LCCN 2022044715 (ebook) | ISBN 9781636280936 (paperback) | ISBN 9781636280943 (ebook)
Subjects: LCGFT: Poetry.
Classification: LCC PS3603.A7345 T73 2023 (print) | LCC PS3603.A7345 (ebook) | DDC 811/.6—dc23/eng/20220928
LC record available at https://lccn.loc.gov/2022044714
LC ebook record available at https://lccn.loc.gov/2022044715

Publication of this book has been made possible in part through the generous financial support of program sponsor James Wilson.

The National Endowment for the Arts, the Los Angeles County Arts Commission, the Ahmanson Foundation, the Dwight Stuart Youth Fund, the Max Factor Family Foundation, the Pasadena Tournament of Roses Foundation, the Pasadena Arts & Culture Commission and the City of Pasadena Cultural Affairs Division, the City of Los Angeles Department of Cultural Affairs, the Audrey & Sydney Irmas Charitable Foundation, the Meta & George Rosenberg Foundation, the Albert and Elaine Borchard Foundation, the Adams Family Foundation, Amazon Literary Partnership, the Sam Francis Foundation, and the Mara W. Breech Foundation partially support Red Hen Press.

First Edition
Published by Red Hen Press
www.redhen.org

for Roberto,
y el hogar que tengo en ti siempre lleno de libros, arte, música, y amor

and with gratitude to all of the visual artists and writers
who have inspired these poems

Contents

II

III

IV

Trace

The Body and Its Rubble

El cuerpo, a labyrinth
        of cicatrizes zig-
zagging through its muddy tierra.
        Suspicious scratches, yellow lumps
invitan la bruja y sus susurros
        o la calaca con un ojo
llena de la luna ámbar,
        el otro de vidrio—evergreen
window refusing to shutter itself.
        What is the timbre of a new wound?
Of a song that stings before scabbing?
        Excavate with me the ruins
of our purple terrain—
        its kingdom of rubble.

I

"If the memory of an event is a 'trace' in the land, the actions that took place long ago are 'etched' there, but 'long ago' may become tomorrow at anytime!"

—Cecilia Vicuña, from *About to Happen*

"Every living being is also a fossil. Within it, all the way down to the microscopic structure of its proteins, it bears the traces if not the stigmata of its ancestry."

—Jacques Monod, from *Chance and Necessity: An Essay on the Natural Philosophy of Modern Biology*, translated by Austryn Wainhouse

Nexus

(after Ana Mendieta's *Silueta* series, earth-body works, 1973–80)

"I have thrown myself into the very elements that produced me,
using the earth as my canvas and my soul as my tools." —Ana Mendieta

This body always compost—
hair a plot of thin green stems
snowing a shroud of petals,
skin mud-sucked to bark,
trunk only timber isthmusing
riverbanks, each finger
a dirty uprooting.

How many stones did I have
to swallow before my legs
believed their own weight?
Dropped into silhouette
of thigh and hip, a ridge
of ossicles crushed to fine
white whispers. Offering Cuilapán

their orphaned pleas, one
twin lingers outside the nave, one
cloistered in a vaulted niche,
its ledge of red roses edging
her blood-soaked robes.
Meat, bone—a deer's skitter
and bolt from the arrow,
an iguana's severed tail, spiny tracks.

They say we dig our own graves.
I have laid me down
in a Yagul tomb, outlined
my island arms with twig, rock,
blossom, mud. My pulse with fire,
glass and blood. I've raised
myself in the earth's beds, left
this trace, this exiled breath.

Cien nombres para la muerte: Las jodidas/The Screwed Ones

(after the drawings *La Jodida, Las Huesos,* and *La Cargona* by Erik Ricardo de Luna Genel)

We are bent from the loads we've carried
strapped to our bony backs—sacks
of maíz, hierbas, frijoles; bundles
of firewood; jerry jugs of precious agua.
Each Saturday, we haul tall stacks
of caged birds to the mercado to sell
their captive songs—their laments,
our heaviest burden.

Hobble a mile in our ragged huaraches,
holes in their tire-tread soles. Follow
us to the village of whispers
where the only gritos belong to the wind,
empty doorways grown over with weeds,
our men's dusty boots waiting years
for their return. Look into the cenotes
of our eyes. You'll find no fish,
no flores, no monedas. Only sacrifices
with their mouths full of mud
and the dread of our itchy grins.

Then tell us you would never risk
wrapping your little lamb in a rebozo,
grabbing your withered staff, and heading
north—devil sun, scorpion, migra
be damned. You'd fly for the birds
whose latches you could not unlock.
You'd fly so the only satchel your daughter
hoists on her shoulders is heavy
with libros, lapices y sueños. You'd fly
never believing they would wrest her
from your back and lock her in a cage.

Cien nombres para la muerte: La hilacha/The Loose Thread

(after a drawing by Erik Ricardo de Luna Genel and
in memory of Óscar Alberto Martínez Ramírez and Valeria)

Ix Chel, skeleton moon at her loom,
wipes her furrowed forehead, daddy
longlegs dangling like loose threads
from the corners of her eyes dark as ditches.
She stitches crossbones into skirts,
weaves skulls into blankets she will trade
with travelers. "Mantillas, rebozos!"
she'll sing, unfurling her wares for parents
to wrap around babes she has guided
from their mothers' oceans to Earth.

Under one moon, a Salvadoran father
and mother cannot wait any longer
in the winding lines of starved
asylum seekers ordered to halt.
So their daughter, not yet two, wraps
her tiny arms around the bough
of papi's neck, clings to his trunk
as he wades into the big river, swims
strong as salmon, against churning currents.

But when he spills her on the bank, warns
her to wait, and lunges back into the torrent
for mami, the little one panics, follows.
Under one sun, the river carries them
away, defying the border
it never meant to become.

Ix Chel's waning crescent finds them
first, face down in the mud,
wrapped together in the black shroud
of papi's shirt. And from her great jug,

holding all the waters of heaven,
she spills storms to wash away
the lines we've carved, dug, drilled,
the walls we've built in chain link, barbed
wire, concrete, and steel between desert
and desert, river
and river, earth
and earth, between father
and mother, mother
and child
under one moon.

Our Lady of Sorrows

(after Ana Mendieta's *Untitled*, Silueta Series, 1980)

has appeared to the mountain
        dwellers, her grief engraved
where stone softens to clay. Keep
        your eyes sharp for a dagger.
In its hilt, you'll find her face
        pressed to the earth's cheek. Kiss
this sacred spot before the rains
        wash it away like her orphaned
feet. Notched heart cradles
        a planet heavy with night-
mares flying into empty mouths.
        Listen for their thirsty murmurs.
She'll push her ponderous child
        into the dew of a San Felipe dawn,
name him Salvador. They'll rest
        beneath a web spun umbilical,
eclipsed from our human eyes.

Our Lady

        stone   clay

                earth
                    rain
                        orphaned

            heart

eclipsed

Psalm

You sit in breath's beat,
hands washed with sage and ash,
circles tattooed
on the padded palms.
This is a psalm for the mouth
that opens in the *om* of your fist
and says nothing
as it stretches
into a psalm for silence,
chatter scattering like mice
when you step
into the vanishing field.
This is a psalm for pollen
drifting in a symphony
you cannot hear, its sex
in every pore, every hair
lifting. This is a psalm for wings,
for the helium and string
that releases you
from yourself. Like water,
this is a psalm for healing
without being held.

Ofrenda de Otoño

A flurry of chickadees unfurls
from birch trees as red fox
loiter in a commune of sunflowers—
zorro scattering xochitl seeds—free-
fall of food we will squirrel
away for the months when snow crags
climb to garage roofs.
Oso, gather your ripe berries. Venado, your red
maple leaves. Murciélago, your mosquitos.
Chapulín, your tiny violins. A traffic
of bitter winds y carámbanos
are knocking at our doors. I offer you
this molcajete de cominos, crushed cloves
y coraje, chile ancho, hechizo de bruja.
This stone has hissed like a radiator,
crackled like a hearth, smoked
like a shell of sweetgrass—una benedicíon.

Cien nombres para la muerte:
La zapatona/The Fleet-Footed Woman

(after a print by Erik Ricardo de Luna Genel and for Daniel)

Brother, your heart was a speed-metal
drummer in a breakaway, jamming
for the finish. They had to trip it, stop
it, start it, shock it till it threw you
to your knees. And La Zapatona, sure-footed
in her winged sneakers, tucked phalanges
into fists and bolted, ponytail sailing
in her wake, piano grin full of keys
hammering sweeps. She shot you
that mal de ojo, all black holes, and you
still smell her sweat, her stale breath,
feel its fire in your lungs. *I cheated her*
three times, you say, *now she sprints*
inside my chest. Now she's neck and neck.

Brother,

(beginning with a line by Robin Reagler)

My pain is a cloud that might be saying goodbye.
It waves its plump little hand and sails
into blue. I imagine a fist pump and wink,
mischievous smirk to rival your Cheshire grin.
It took a year before I began
to wake without memory of missing
your last words because by the time I arrived,
they had all flown north
in search of a cool lake breeze rustling
between Aspens, the loon's Llorona wail
ghosting midnight's misty waves,
knotty pine walls of the tiny room
where we slept three to a bed
comforted by dim yellow light shining
through cracks and by sounds of our parents,
grandparents drinking beer and slapping cards
down on the oilcloth just outside
the drawn curtain we pretended was a door.

Ofrenda for Daniel

as if laying a new braid of sweet-
grass in your birchbark basket,

as if dusting off your picture
when sun streams past your eyes,

as if rattling the baby gourd
maracas surrounding you

as if whistling "Blackbird" softly
in the dead of night

as if wrapping myself in your empty
jacket, its sleeves reaching

beyond my fingertips
as if marigolds, marigolds, marigolds

as if filling the kitchen with scents
of chile y chocolate

as if sugar skulls and pan
de muerto on your birthday

as if playing your voice again
on the answering machine

as if sliding the silken braid
of your hair through my fingers

as if sounding your name,
as if you never left.

In Veiled Voices

(after Harvey K. Littleton's blown glass, *Conical Intersection*, 1985)

Topple a mountain's cool crown
cool mount
into the tangerine sunset,
set into

dusk's cobalt claw snagged
snagged light
in its honey slump crawl
awl slump

across dunes. Petrify a gush
gush across
of silt and shale. Fix mud
mud silt

with ash. Magenta mesas stretch
stretch ash
between stars, meet 300-foot
meet between

drops to the canyon floor. Cliff-
cliff drops
dwellers, a red clay bowl nestles
red dwellers

in the belly of its own ghost. Come,
Come in
the blistering stones speak.
speak the

Time to grind the yellow corn,

yellow time

prepare this tilted table, push

push tilted

our elliptical breath

breath our

through amber spheres of light.

light through

On the Coast in Pedasí

Beachedboats litter coves,
        sails sprawled like abandoned skirts
of lovers asleep on the sand.
        The empty zócalo simmers—
a secret waiting
        to be whispered,
Café Tiesto's shutters and doors
        anchored open to release
its brick-oven heat. Through
        a streaked windshield,
you watch a woman sweep
        the dusty veranda,
wipe tables spruced
        with buds drooping
into an afternoon still
        as a breath held.

If you exhale now, a tornado
        of bees will careen
around the corner,   swarm
the plaza,   blackening its sky.
        The woman will drift
inside,   gently latch shutters
        as the funnel cloud
                drones
        through town,   busy
        with the work
of finding home.   Once the horizon
        has swallowed all of them,
you will part your lips,
        release the locks,
                exit cover.   Watch

your step.   Every migration
bears its fallen,
        those that drop
                to the dirt.
Across the plaza, the woman will push
        the door   open
hum as she sweeps.

Thin Air

Trapped by a bend
in the basilica, a bird
hums inside at the humming-
bird outside, glass trilling
against its frenzied whir.

A man I'll never stop
loving climbs the wall,
hovers on a sill stretching
to grasp at anxious
reflections. How many

heartbeats to escape inside
the outside of joy? To turn
a green wing toward
his dark palm closing
off light? Lightly palms globe

the terror song, carry it
to a garden like a sacred stone.
On a holy hill that keeps
our crutches, fingers unfurl
in a lemniscate of wings.

Still Life

That morning, we shut all the windows,
locked the doors behind us and took off,
gliding along freeways connected to curvy
country roads where we could stop,
untangle ourselves from seatbelts and break
into a run across the sap-green meadow,
then tumble to earth panting, sucking air
into our natural ventilators, healthy homes.

The next day, all that freedom
drained out of my face when I flew
upstairs into the bath, flung open
the shower curtain and found a tiny
sparrow in the tub, dead as a still life,
once trapped and tired enough to plummet
to porcelain spotted with specks of water.

How could we have let it in without notice?
How can I toss it after imagining
its frenzied flight from room to room,
window to window, bed to dresser,
book to alarm clock? How can I call it, *it?*
How could we? How can I?

Shadow Dancing with the Living and the Dead

(after Roy Staab's *Shadow Dance* installation at Villa Terrace, Milwaukee, WI, 2016, for Soham Patel and Milwaukee's twenty-four homicide victims, August 2016)

Flexing like acrobats, twined reeds bend
into six mammoth rings. Anchored
willow branches shoulder this universe,
its planets entering each other's orbits.
A bent line is stronger than a straight one.

Approach, and ellipses shift to circles
locking arms with their shadows
while blocks and worlds away, men orphan
themselves, tear through one another.

When we enter the constellation, it turns
to labyrinth, spiders stretching sky
bridges from branch to branch, swallow tails
drifting between loops, lawn beginning

its journey back to prairie where I lie
in a crescent-moon nest. Nearby, fists grip
clubs, train triggers to split and shatter, break
ground for graves, never enough jute
to suture ourselves together.

Soon birds will tug at twine, insects
eat of the hairy reeds. Winds may loosen
and sunder. But today, you have found
your way to the center. When I meet you
where you stand, our shadows intersect.

Ghost Species

Pockets of this city resist its grit, open
        portals that travel   back-
wards   to a wilderland
        we can only imagine   rewound

many decades north   where dragonflies
        are the lone   black points   on the horizon
swallows of light skimming the lake—

where fireflies gather   in small galaxies
        milky ways of bulbous bodies flashing   on/
off   like lit entrances to exotic dance   strip
        tease   in a hidden acre of woods.

Pockets of this city   shape-
        shift   to meadow   bracken pond   wild arbor
summon their disappeared to a ghost dance

where fat raccoons tumble across midnight's front lawns,
deer   scatter
                among abandoned bulldozers, dump trucks,

summoning geese to form blockades
in the street,   stare drivers down.

        Concrete is not an object
        for chipmunks tearing fault   lines in garage floors.

                Coyotes cross bicycle paths at dusk,
                        slink into shadow,
                                tear rabbits to shrieks   on the patio
                                beneath our bedroom window

while we dream   of a crib long stored in the attic
        or sent away   to a young mother   grown old.

What can we do with this gathering of ghosts
                                                  but welcome them home,
for they've returned all at once   bright as a quintet of monarchs
                                    in milkweed flickering.

Chiral Formation

(palindrome after Roy Staab's 2012 installation on
Little Lake, Lynden Sculpture Garden, Milwaukee, WI)

Buckthorn saplings curve
into hoops, linking boughs.
Ring around the rosy.

Four staked crowns etch
surface. Barbed shiver.
Pocket full of hands.

What do you net
in the intersect
when you walk on water?

A forest, my haunted face
crowing, cumulous algae?
Our ashes, child slim as a reed?

Where does a lemniscate drift,
chiral twin wander
when the sun falls down?

down falls sun
wander in chiral
drift scate where

reed child our
cumulous crowing
haunt my forest.

water walk
in sect
do what?

full pock
barbed face
etch own ake

rosy round ing
ink oops
pling.

Lampyridae

Nightfall lures
solar glow
lighting a foot-

path at woods'
entrance. After you
pass the last bulb,

tap ground in front
of you to check
for roots, reach

a hand into black
to block brambles'
scratch, until eyes

adjust to the outline
of your fingers,
profile of my mouth,

lips open to catch—
stop—the sound
of my breath.

In a clearing,
campfire sparks?
Burning brush?

No, thousands
of fireflies
blinking, flickers

of the forest's
secrets no one
would believe.

Catch and Release

Turn over
        with the slap
of the undertow,
boat, your creaky bed.
        Wake   lapping pier.
A lake links two lands,
anchors shore to shore.
        You'll cross this isthmus.
towing a forest. Drift
        past the tangled lines.

❧

bucktail
        pitch and dance
        thrash and switch
surface   twitcher
        cast   shimmy
jerk and reel
        slip   spot
snag and tug
reel, reel, reel
                heave

❧

Flush the gills with lake.
        Follow scales
until they flicker   vanish
        swathed in the clot
of thickening weeds.
What cell will save us

from the flashy lure?
Will our bellies bloom
anemone and coral
in the hands that wrestle us
from hoop   to hull,
keep them so full of the catch
that they measure
and release,
drag a net packed with nothing
to the shore?

Yegua's Daughter

(after Ana Mendieta's triptych *On Giving Life*, 1975)

"I will fasten sinews on you, bring flesh upon you, overlay you with skin, and put breath in you, and you shall live . . ." (Ezekiel 37:1–10)

I.

Long before pressing my ribs to his,
I covered Osain's face and hands
with plasticine. Smoothed it
from cranium to mandible, pausing
to plant a seed beneath each closed lid.
Slitting open nose and mouth, I cleared
a path for the winds of Olódùmarè.
Specks of clay splashed his breastbone
like flecks of blood, scraps of meat
as I webbed one finger to the next,
flexed knuckles to crease the unworked
sinew, and tucked rills in his palms
moistened by dew. Some would call it
a baptism.

II.

Others, a wedding. If you look past
my belly's swollen lip, you'll see me
slip a ring on Osain's finger, rub
his palm like a smooth stone.
This before the kiss that seals us,
before I mount his bleached esqueleto,
iliac crest cupping my hips, bluff
of buttocks, grass gushing between thighs.
If you reach into the frame, you can
pluck a reed, rub it between thumbs,
make it whistle.

III.
His sacrum tattoos a crescent moon
on my belly. Can you feel the knots—
my fallopian antlers, his knees?
Sweat dripping from my forehead
splashes into his mask, its pink fossa
swallowing my face. You ask why
I do not fear slipping away
with the Eggun. Pués, díme,
if you could be a bellows, blow
air into the earth's collapsing lungs,
wouldn't you?

Inverse

(after Amy Cropper's *Inverse*, painted ash and hawthorn, 2011, Lynden Sculpture Garden, Milwaukee, WI, and Ana Mendieta's *Body Tracks*, paintings, 1982)

Cropper stripped the Hawthorne
 of its skin, excised
arms, painted its flayed torso
 fire-engine red
until the tree blazed—a squat flame
 igniting weeds, yellow
leaves, snow piling
 in its lap. All year long,
naked boughs glistened
 like a flock of bloody wings.

But when May pushes green
 through cracked wood,
blossoms bursting from a torch
 of lacquered limbs, I wait
for Ana Mendieta to step
 out of the knotted wood,
trunk simmering, arms raised
 in the V of free-
fall to our knees, broken
 stems regenerating.

Against Insularity

Let us push air into our splenetic bubbles,
until they contain brimming worlds
we can plunge into—blood-orange
skies tinged with lavender beyond the horizon
we've never traversed, across the line
we've never transgressed. Time to purge
our stampeding litanies, pistol-whipped plans
sutured to impossible futures, manacled
to metal desks and manicured lawns.

Be with me a forest of deciduous trees—
lizard-wrinkled, century of rings rising
to silver-streaked clouds.
All our granular wreckage, our tin-pan scraps
are bursting with veridian tympany.
Light the cosmic fire, feed it with lungs
the size of ships' bellows. Spark celestial candles.
They will cluster into amethyst constellations
like the lilacs we were born to be.

II

"One can find traces of every life in each life."
—Susan Griffin, from *A Chorus of Stones: The Private Life of War*

Because We Come from Everything

(a collage poem after a line by Juan Felipe Herrera and using only language from books by Mexican American and Native American authors whose publications were removed from Tucson Public School classrooms under the school district's 2010 law HB 2281, since overturned)

Because we come from everything—
from zero; from a doubt slender as a hair;
from a land of travelers, wanderers
and its geography of scars; from frayed edges
and muddy hems; from the border sealed
tight as an envelope—Meskin/Dixon/line.

Because we come from Operation Wetback,
Operation Peter Pan, Operation Gatekeeper;
floodlights, sensors, infrared spy videos,
night vision camera, topo maps, helicopters,
and holding cells; from sharpshooting
goose-steppers round every corner;
from alien gods and alien names
and alien eyes and wild alien tongues;
from the barbed wire politics of stupidity.

Because we come from the ship
that will never dock;
from a parallel universe,
double helix, synchronized sigh,
the infinite division del secreto terrible,
the screaming sun.

Because we come from steel mill smoke
and silt slaughtering the sky;
a matchbox house beneath the shadow
of the freeway, windows so small you'd think
they were holding their breath
and roaches so big they look Pleistocene,
kids hopscotching on the sidewalk
and a dusty, unpaved road called Sal Si Puedes.

Because we come from the geometry of disaster,
schools torn down and sold for scrap,
bristled restrictions and chuco hieroglyphics,
the gash sewn back into a snarl,
crushed cigarette in a glass.

Because we come from lineoleum and formica;
from rooms boarded shut and rented to strangers
en una esquina aparte de los demás,
hole in the ceiling, kids on milk crates,
the hammerhead of responsibility,
tin plate face down on the floor.

We come from brujas, chavalas, carnales,
cabrones, rucas, locas, comadres, los vatos, los
perros, y los perididos, una vieja
y sus recuerdos, eternal ciphers with voices
bright as chrome. Because we come
from every cell, every follicle, every nerve,
the petals of the body, an orchid of blood,
mapped birthmarks, knowing and unknowing.

Because we come from museums and waiting
rooms—hostile territory and collateral damage,
Because we come from the Out-of-Service Area,
from another bad dream, a bowl of beings.
Because we come from el Rasquache—
Tex-Mex with a Brooklyn accent,
Santería Tupperware party,
magnet car-statuettes and kitsch calendar art
at the flea market, la segunda,
from the word "cachivaches,"
and la lotería—a world loaded on each back.

Because we come from everything
on top of everything; from unbending dreams
and a long line of eloquent illiterates,
the throat that must clear itself
and apologize each time it speaks—
a sound like swallowing mud.
Because we come from el camino
de la mestiza—the path of red and black ink,
from linguistic terrorism and literary archaeologists;
from each of the star's stories.
Because we come from a green flutter,
the hummingbird's throat;
a chorus resounding for acres.

Because we come from dichos,
cantos, cuentos; from the spoken word—
the seed of love in the darkness.

Ars Resistencia

(inspired by the art of El Anatsui and the Border Arts Workshop)

Fish bottle caps from heaps
of distillery waste. Sift trash
for milk tin lids. Twist, crush, chain-
link them to each other
like thousands of small arms
locking. Drape them
into fifteen-by-thirty-foot seas
of kente cloth, tapestry, grass-
lands swagged in wind,
speckled with red wings,
blue-silver agama.

Do this in communion with others.
Urge them to reshape landscape,
shift peaks and folds.
Call it salvage, reuse, synergetic upcycle.
Call it recover and reclaim.
Call it puro rasquache, güey.

Do this in memory of
net-work, warp and weft.
Twist and distort text-
ure. Strike the loom.

Do this in memory of
painted deserts we walked through
in a pre-wall, wireless world
rolling before us like the sea.

Make yourself so small, the cuffs
fall from your wrists. Then thread
the warp. Climb, crawl.

Drag your dinner table a la frontera.
Set one end acá en México, el otro allá.
Prepare posole with all the fixings.
Invita a tus amigos de ambos lados.
Claro, Adelita will ask Paul to pass
the heat—*los jalapeños y rábanos,*
por favor. Pero la migra will be waiting,
watchando. Y cuando Paul's pinky
sneaks over the line,
they may not let him back
in, ese. He'll have to swim or sprint.
The least you can do is bring
him some aguacate, un poquito
de cilantro. Show us your fancy foot-
work, your disappearing act:
Now you're here. Ahora ________

Storm tomato fields, spitting
fricatives, snapping
toxic vines. Slingshot
plosives at orange groves
dropping citrus
into the blistered hands reaching
to pick it Up the anti.
Plant your syllables on picket lines.
Pace Plant your selves in public
space. Refuse to flinch. Plant
feet so firm, will takes root. Plant will
so wide, ears sprout ancestral maize.

Eat of this body, unengineered.
Do this in memory of

corn, potatoes, papaya, squash
tomatoes, cotton, canola, soy
beets, zucchini, cane.

Do this in memory of
milkweed's monarchs, honey bees.

Do this in memory of
water   your last sip.

Paint the winter white howl.
Inscribe the undivided *o*.
Sound the voiced and voiceless stops
of hunger strike
of boycott's broken shackles
de calacas with their midnight carcajadas
waking us from sleep.

Placa/Roll Call

(after Charles "Chaz" Bojórquez's *Placa/Roll Call,* 1980)

"If the city was a body, graffiti would tell us where it hurts."
—Chaz Bojórquez

And this block would shout, "Nos diste un CHINGAZO, cabrón. Mira esta cara rota, these baton-cracked ribs, this black-and-blue street dizzy con gente: BLADES, KIKI, LARRY, SNOW, ENRIQUE, CONNIE, ELTON, KING, DAVID, KELLY, JEFF, RAT'ON, CHAZ, los de aquí, los de abajo. This roll call won't be silenced, not by Glock, not by chokehold. This is our temple of runes, our tomb—its glyphic curve and flow, calligraphic code writ acrylic. This, our relic, our scroll unrolled in catacombs, our flecks of subtext still buzzing después de que vayamos con La Pelona. ¡QUE LUCHA, LOCO! Ven, baila con nostros to the aerosol's maraca y hiss, al punk en español's furious sweat. Hang your head out the window y dale un grito tan lleno de duende that it cracks the pavement, summons our dead to dinner. Turn the tonal kaleidoscope. Then pause, catch your breath, so you don't miss the illegible moment where all the mystery lives. There, de-cypher *that!*"

Public Promise

(after Julian Correa's *Mixed Media on Canvas*, 2007)

P is for pigsty
    blood-splashed underpass
    incarcerated spatter
    public sky, privatized
    pistols, ink-washed glyph talk.

P is for paint can
    pregnant with probable cause
    plosive as Pleiades
    poised to punk the sky
    with a phatter punctuation.

P is for pollos y sus puños
    snapped to the steel rail.
    Prayer drizzles down pilings
    while Malinche points
    to pocked promises, empty lots.

P is for prophets bull-whipped
    in the oppidan jungle.
    Purple mountains rise
    in the pits of their stomachs
    and from their peyote tongues,

    phosphorescent scrolls.

Punk en Español

Embrace the skunky ruckus:
        electric guitars and scream-growls
gritando a los brazos agitados,
        kicked shins, bruised butts,
cleaving montones de carne
        in the moshpit. This music's missive
summersaults, sparks,
        ignites, crackles volcanic
because the world
is broken anyway—
        a flipped vehicle, dim debris
ablaze. Quién no entiende
        the griot's bullet blasts
shrieking "¡asesinos!"? Wrecking ball
        of angry abandon, golpes tiernos.
This circle of bent bone—
        its own communion,
raucous cariño llorando.

#Petrochemicals

"One Word: Plastics." —*The Graduate,* 1967

Plastic pacifier, pastel ring of keys.
Plastic bassinette, playpen, baby bottle.
Pink plastic barrettes, balloons, big red ball.
Plastic swimming pool, PlaySkool.
Little plastic stove, fried eggs, butter melt-
ing in the plastic pan. Plastic jack-o'-lantern
begging for individually plastic-wrapped
candies. Plastic water wings, plastic pail
and shovel to scoop plastic-coated
sand next to the plastic ocean.

Plastic straws in plastic milk shake cups.
Plastic carnival prizes, Legos, snow globes.
Plastic helmets, skateboards, rackets.
Plastic pens, paper-keepers, headphones.
Plastic toothbrushes, shavers, tubes
between Q-tips. Plastic strawberry lip gloss,
plastic Blossom and Bloom shampoo, vanilla
hand soap, plastic Barbie body, plastic skin
and preteen wishes for plastic surgery.

Plastic milk cartons—one per week—
millions per week. Plastic mayonnaise,
ketchup, mustard. Plastic serving tray,
plates, plastic forks, knives, and spoons
wrapped in plastic to eat plastic
hamburgers and sip plastic Pepsis
right out of the plastic cooler.

Giving you a headache? Plastic bottle
of Excedrin, plastic-coated capsules
and a plastic cup of water to lube

your plastic joints. Put on your plastic
eyeglasses to find them. At the store,
a plastic bag for each lemon, bunch
of broccoli, handful of brussels sprouts,
for the single tomato. Paid for with plastic
and all packed loosely between plastic smiles
in ever more plastic bags.

Our Teeming Shores

When Earth gasps, the moon drinks
our planet's lost energy and inches
farther and farther away. Each year,
her shine fading a shade, her pull
weakening until she might loosen
her grasp, let us go. Until she might escape
our footprints lingering for centuries,
our satellites crashing into her,
our spent rockets, dead power packs,
ultraviolet cameras, family photos wrapped
in plastic, diamond pins, golf balls, flags,
shovels, ladders, towels, boots, food
wrappers, dirty wet wipes, human ashes,
ninety-six trash bags full of human waste.
The moon backs away inch by inch
until she might stop us from searching
for her water as ours evaporates, halt
our profitable plans to build bubbles
in her craters and mine metal and mineral,
every rare element we can extract.
Yes, each year the moon places her lips
on Earth's mouth, draws a breath,
and slips away from the wretched
refuse of our teeming shores.

Sand Baggers' Knockdown

("Turtle Dead After Severely Beaten on Golf Course," June 12, 2013)

Only to perch on sun-soaked logs,
to migrate or nest,
will a snapping turtle leave water.
Only for eggs that evolved
40 million years ago
will she plod through the rough,
drag her dinosaur tail and wrinkled chins
across fairways to the open sand
trap where the hackers tee off.
Chelydra Serpentina's tiger-striped eyes
can see straight above her,
watch the five-iron lunge
at her head before cracking chinks,
busting bloody holes in her carapace.

Still, she will not budge,
this olive-skinned mother
whose ancestors survived
a six-mile-wide meteorite blitz,
its nuclear winter, the end of an age;
this elder whose forebear faced
the great flood and offered the world
her back—bludgeoned to death
in a Wisconsin bunker. The cold-blooded
creature had blocked the man's chip shot,
his chance at a birdie, bragging rights,
and a round of High Life
for the losers at the bar.

Trespassing

Near Lac Courte Oreilles, ten of us
slept in bedrolls on a farmhouse's
sprawling attic floor. There to trespass
on land stolen by a subsidiary
of a subsidiary of the largest
mining company in the world,
to get arrested, to stop the drilling
for one more day. I remember nothing

about the protest except the No
Parking signs for long stretches
of county road leading to the site.
Can't tell you how I managed
to cross the line without arrest.
Can't tell you the names
of compatriots; colors of their eyes,
hair, skin; slogans decaled across
their tees or how many days
we stayed. What I can tell you

is that five of us woke at 4:00 a.m.,
laced up our hiking boots,
slipped on coats, hats, gloves
and walked into the forest
before dawn. For fifteen minutes,
hoarfrost draped diamonds
onto every tree branch, crystals
onto every bush's crown, each ridge
on the snowy trail shimmering.
Hoarfrost bathed us in iridescence.

I stood there in the world
until the sun began to rise
and stars to melt, drop
at my feet. This is all
I've remembered forever
about that time, that place.

Top Fifteen Reasons Mexicans Love Tortillas

(after Natalie Diaz's "Top Ten Reasons Indians Are Good at Basketball")

Because están hechos de La Diosa Maíz.
Because they are the spoon and fork rolled up in one.
Because we can wipe our mouths with them
when we run out of napkins.
Because slapping the masa from hand to hand
reminds us of playing pattycake with our babies,
now too grown up for our silly games.
Because we toss them directly on the gas
burner and flip them quickly as a spark
with our fingertips, no pots or pans necessary.
Because when they hit the comal,
little air pockets in the masa puff up
with hope like hills in flat endless deserts
or bubblegum and balloons on our birthdays.
Because they taste like the clouds
of heaven the nuns tell us we will sleep
on if we learn to form our "t's"
between our teeth with a sharp bite.
Because pools of butter melt
in their valleys and run down our chins
as we clutch them in one hand
while we shoot hoops with the other.
Because nuestras madres y abuelas
pasan todo el día piling them in columns
on their red Formica tabletops.
Because our fathers tell us how they hated
making tortilla deliveries from their coaster wagons
when they were boys and abuela sold the delicacies
to neighbors for a quarter per dozen.
Because, como un año al próximo, they are circles.
Because our eyes feast on golden wheat fields,
and our stories speak of yellow, blue, burgundy,

brown, black kernels spilling from baskets
before the Corporate Almighty outlawed
all but one variety. Because cornrows are not
only in our hair, but in our backyards.
Because our bisabuela's bisabuela's bisabuela
dried the kernels, soaked them in lime and water,
ground them in molcajetes bigger
than our heads, worked the dough
until small round cakes lay in their hands.
Because they started from scratch.

III

"The bodyprint
is an illegible surge:
of leaving trace
of self en route"
—Carmen Giménez Smith, from "A Devil Inside Me," *Milk and Filth*

Below

Dragonfly in flexible splendor lifts
aloof off the pier. Skims
the surface like I do afraid
of seaweed tentacles,
jagged rocks, leeches
underneath, a wrinkle
in mistaken identity, doppleganger
weighted with chains
at the bottom of a glacial lake.
What can I tell you of unlucky knee twists,
slips on slimy stones in the shallows,
of canoe flips, bruises
blooming from the corner of a snarl?
When the surface shimmers
do you wonder which crimes linger
beneath a floating oar?
Some cattails are invasive species.
If we machete them down, they will
grow taller next year. When we dig
out the fickle roots, what oozes
between our suspicious toes?
Which sediments compose
the palpable strata,
each rusty layer that has made us?

Bucketsful

When I was a child, I had a rusty bucket-
ful of ochre wonder, of mustard seed
and yarrow, jasper stone and finch
feather, of butterscotch and hopscotch,
botched tongues and dizzy syntax.

Bullies dumped it all over the sidewalk,
their pimpled hiccups echoing
under overpasses while pigeons pecked
at the granular wreckage, and the finch
feather flew south in search of its bird.

Others stuffed my bucket with snarls
and suffocating toadlets, ravenous
revulsion and arrogant sermons.
One held a bucketful of Jesus to the sky,
and the buckets multiplied.

I snuck away with the ugly bucket
scratched by stars, dented by dark clouds,
the lonely one ready to carry friends
like shells and seeds, water and bone,
caterpillars, ladybugs, mud and stone.

Under Water

We didn't anticipate rust. How it could climb walls, eat eaves, chew holes in the roof that blistering July we submerged mom's vintage tin Colonial, flooding its retro rooms, '40s suburbia sinking like a submarine to the bottom of our plastic pool. We never imagined splotches of red-orange dust would splash like an action painting above the mantel, drip down the lithographed curtains.

Ours was the era of Hula-Hoops, Ouija boards, and twisting limbs across a mat of giant polka-dots. After shows like *Lost in Space* and *Hello Down There*, we played underwater sea family. Pink crib and playpen floated about the nursery while plastic parents swam from room to room trying to catch their bobbling toddlers. Then the mom drifted downstairs to load her wringer washing machine. Dad to the john, always overflowing. Neighbors thought nothing of diving through open windows to deliver seaweed pie or return baby brother whose lullaby had carried him off in the current when we were busy holding down the refrigerator, stove, and six kitchen chairs. Underwater sea kids would never have to dry dishes or scrub behind their ears. No dusting, sweeping, mopping: Paradise in two and a half feet of water. *Way down below the ocean, where I want to be, she may be.* Even decided to use our goldfish for the family pet, but when chlorine killed Fido, we settled for a rubber barracuda. The proportions weren't right—sort of like the Flintstones with a dinosaur for a dog. But the ocean made monstrous claims anyway: prehistoric hagfish, mermaids, selkies. Who knew what might be possible?

In November, when the first snow fell and mom stormed the garage for a shovel, she found her Cold War childhood cracked and leaning like a Mississippi shack in the corner. Ruined. In the gloom of all our soggy faces, who knew we'd grow up to live in a whole neighborhood of underwater houses? That crustaceous sea people would emerge from the waves with their fins tucked in and walk away, as if occupying land for the first time?

Miniature Witch

In my miniature autumn village
where clock towers perpetually strike
midnight, all roofs are thick with thatch,
a loose piece of straw whirling
to bald grass whenever the furnace kicks on.
I stacked a pile of quarter-inch pumpkins
in each yard strewn with tiny oak leaves,
but the streetlamps I ordered
from a catalog were too small and refused
to stand up, so the village is dark
but for pinprick orange lights strung
from roof to roof. No village exists
without animals, so I invited
a white rabbit, gray squirrel, and red fox
itty-bitty as breadcrumbs
to scamper beneath windows or stretch out
in the meadow beyond my buffet's mirror.
Glass ghosts smaller than thimbles gather
beneath red maples near the pond
I walked to at eight years old with a froglet
I'd nurtured from tadpole, finally ready
to be released into slimy, wet liberation.
It barely felt the mud between toes
when dirty boys fishing nearby scooped
it up, speared it with a hook,
and dropped it into the gaping maw of a carp.
Yesterday, our mailman finally delivered
the package I'd been expecting for months.
I unwrapped the dime-sized polymer witch,
her tiny cauldron falling from my pinched fingers
into a thicket of cattails that threaten to choke
the pocket-sized pond. There she hides,

spying the fisherboys who hear her cackle.
They suspect a crow while searching the sky
empty of black wings. Then in his peripheral
vision, the meanest boy spots the broom
I fashioned from scraps of twig and sagebrush
leaning against the craggiest tree. He swears
he saw it whisk the path of curled leaves,
then lift and disappear into the brush
much too close to his spine.

Rupture

(after Remedios Varo's painting *Ruptura*, 1955)

The Carmelite folds like a bat
into her ochre wings. Eyes
from all six windows conspire
flight, cloistered gaze shifting
in a suspicious wind. Everything
curls into this spectral eve: snails
coiling from the veins of leaves,
curtains unlashing—sprung tongues.
Released, a flurry of onion-skin spells
flock to lips. Whose vow will break
against an orange sky? Whose swoop
and whir, whose murmur?
Sister is a closed umbrella
gathering thunder in the V of her cloak,
a storm in her singular step.

Body as Torture Chamber

Each moon in my fallopian wilderness,
flint scraped against the walls of womb,
stabbed, and doubled me over. Spike
behind my eyes drove all the color
from cheeks, hands and feet numbed.
I wanted to wretch, wore a smock
because I thought I looked pregnant,
all swollen and worried a tarpit
would open beneath my school desk,
swallow me whole, tween boys
circling the perimeter: "Wow!"
"Cool!" "Is she in the basement?"
"No, she fell into hell," their gaping
mouths scrunching into a choral
"Eww," as thick bubbles splotched
the morass. They'd inch closer to the edge,
step gingerly as they checked
crumbling linoleum beneath their toes
when I'd push a fist full of fingers
through the coagulated swamp,
grab an ankle, yanking one little fawn
into the furnace with me. We'd both sink
wicked, and he would know the gnawing
teeth, the ballpeen hammer
to the forehead I felt every moon.

Sweet Sixteen

Sweet sixteen in patched Levi jeans
and spaghetti strap tees, we walked
a mile to meet the bad boys kicking back
at the park, Newports nearly tumbling
from their bottom lips as they flicked
wheels to flint and waited for a spark.

We strolled in with six-packs
of Pabst and sass, asking for a joint
and a motorcycle ride, secretly wishing
for a date to the carnival or concert
or next beer bash. But we barely popped
the tops of our cans, had any chance
to joke or flirt or speak of summer plans
before dusk deepened to dark, before

he pressed me against tree bark, tightened
his vice of a body to mine, and grew
ten hands that grabbed everywhere,
even the hair at the back of my head to stop
my thrashing neck. By some dumb luck,
he could not trap my ten-alarm screech,
its siren rupturing his will.

Still, I often wake straining and mute,
knowing either he or the tree will swallow
me if I cannot scream. And what of her?
The one who breezed into the park with me
that summer eve, all cherry lip gloss
and glitter eyes, all cool façade melting
on the inside, all sweet sixteen
with her firefly heart waiting to spark.

Helpless

When bar age was eighteen, I bellied up
at sixteen, ordered VO and water because
VO was from Canada like Neil Young.
Toasted fellow kitchen workers, then spun
and winked at tattooed men who rode
their Harleys straight up to the front door.
Pretty soon, motorcycle mama thighs
hugged a hog, arms wrapped a strapping
chest, and we flew.

How didn't I die—
drunk stuck to a drunk in a city of drunks,
scrambling over fences, darting into alleys
to escape cops, banging on windows
of strange cars parked at the frozen lake
in the middle of the night to hitch a ride
and invite black cadillacs, purple microdot
into our basement for days lost and leaving
us helpless, helpless, helpless, helpless.

This Is Why

At dusk, we pulled and shoved
a patio table beneath cousin's bedroom
window, then yawned a lot as we sat
on the couch with her dad pretending
to nod off to the evening news.
I almost said, "It's been a long day,"
but realized that would be too much
sevventeen-year-old-going-on-fifty
for uncle to believe.

We snuck off to bed where we changed
into patched Levis, Marijuana Pickers
Local No. 13 T-shirts, and Earth shoes.
I slid out the window first, almost toppling
the picnic table with my clumsy landing,
cousin behind me already laughing.
To the park for our weekly search, crossing
fingers that someone had dropped
their bag of weed or flicked their fat joint
when the cops circled for the second time.

Of course, we never found the goods
lying in the grass, but we found friends
with pockets full of other secrets
that we hid beneath our tongues
until they melted. Later, when adults ask,
"Why, why would you be so reckless?"
I describe the ease of pulling myself
back up to the window ledge, gently
tumbling into bed, pulling the blanket
up to my chin as a bluster rustled
dry leaves in the sill. I explain

how I watched three pairs of orange-
and pink-tinged maple leaves swirl
to my feet. How they unwrinkled themselves,
stood up tall, one in each couple bowing
before they raised their hands, touched
fingertips, and began to waltz to Tchaikovsky,
tangerine skirts twirling into yellow. How
elegant the soiree I witnessed at my feet.
"Why would you miss *that?*" I ask.

Sisters

(for Michele, Janet, Reneé, and Jeanne)

I have gotten so tangled in construction cones,
growling yellow machines, and orange-chested men,
that I've veered onto the wrong side of the highway,
cement barricades blocking me from veering back
to the safe side until seconds before twisted metal
and blackout, my sister not screaming or fainting,
but picking the thread of the conversation right
back up as though we had only blinked.

See, my sister is a sister of another sister,
and we don't leave the weave of each other's minds
easily. My sister is a rowboat rocking against shore,
waiting for me to wake, unmoor us from the dock.
My sister is a clay box full of secrets—the kind
you find tucked in a seashell's curve or hand-
written note folded into a triangle. The kind
she whispers in a language only sisters can decode.

She brings good news, waits by my side
for the bad news. My sister helps me pack, drives
the truck stuffed with my failures home and unpacks
them all. She is the one who helps me lift words
heavy as coffins. She keeps me moving. She keeps.
Her conch shell calls all our sisters to the shores
of rising waters, oil slicking the surface, to clean up
the mess we have made of the sister who birthed us all.

Laughing with You

(for Reneé)

is like riding a Tilt-A-Whirl—
stomach clenched, arms wide
open. Like an infinite tickle—
no stops, train spewing tracks in its wake,
losing its caboose.

It's like the best flying dreams
when you swish into canyons, soar
over peaks. Like being shot
out of a cannon straight up to the moon,
like hanging a star
from its crescent tip.

Laughing with you turns me
into trapeze artist, contortionist,
upsidedown, insideout, wracked
with sweet pain, sweat, snot, tears.

It picks all the locks, breaks the chains,
opens every window, bursts
the whole bottle of bubbles.

Laughing with you is being lost
right here, right now,
and not needing to find
my way home.

Coco Pie Road

I jot down directions my mother-in-law
gives us to drive from the dark ocean
road that harbors her beach
house to a buzzed-up blaze of highway.
As my husband steers, I keep
my eyes peeled and warn, *She said*
to turn left on Coco Pie Road.
He throws his head back and laughs,
Concord Pike Road. My mother-in-law's accent
is my grandfather's permitting me
to taste *jus' a lily bit* of beer
on a sweltering August Day.

I close my eyes and wish to wake
at a painted rainbow with a big red arrow
pointing down Coco Pie Road
where the ocean tastes like coconut cream
and bakeries await us on every corner.
Not only do they serve the sweetest pies,
but they build *sangwiches* just like my father
pronounced them on hard rolls
with jamón, lechuga y tomate.
If you criticized my mother's cooking
or wronged her in anyway,
you were an *ass-pipe,* no wipe
nearby to clean the caca off your nose,

and although I kept so many
of their lessons and words piled
on the Formica table of my inner kitchen,
I learned to make *sangwiches*
de spit y vinegar, to swear bilingually,

No me chinges, asspipe! and took pride
in my mispronunciation of *Catholikism,*
while I dodged Sunday school in parks
and alleys. My father prophesied
that this would ruin my life
because God *in-come-passes*
everything, but little does he know
that at the fork, I turned left
down Coco Pie Road, and it smells
like xocoatl spiced with chile
y vanilla, frothy drink of the Gods.

Misdirection

As a child on a neighborhood walk
with my mother, I asked her
which direction we were travelling.
When she answered, "South,"
my eyebrows crinkled confounded.
I thought we were headed north—
thought north was always in front of us
because it's on top of all the maps.
My brothers still ask me if I've arrived
at the North Pole yet. Even now,

if you spin me around a few times
or take me away from Lake Michigan,
I become the compass that has lost
its magnet, the one penguin that strayed
from the colony only to find herself alone
wandering the white sea-sky
with no idea which way to waddle.

On a trip to Fort Atkinson,
I accidentally typed the correct address
in my Google maps, but placed it
in Fond du Lac. Landed at a dead end
in an industrial cul-de-sac, couldn't
figure out what was wrong until my brain
turned on and my phone ran down
to 3 percent. Had to call for directions
on desolate country roads to get
from one "effin'" town to the other.

When I was five, mom made me march
in the Fourth of July buggy parade.
I timidly took my place in line,
wheeled my doll to the route's end
where I promptly got lost
in the crowd of kids skipping off
to their parents, stood crying
beneath a maple tree, helicopter
seeds in my hair, until a policeman
walked me home right across the street.

Now that I've found my way
through four cities, ten apartments,
and two houses all the way back
to my first home, my new home
across the street from the park,
I guess I'm not lost at all.

Keys

My uncle and aunt left me two hands
full of keys, some to lost padlocks,
some so worn, they no longer turn
in locks that block me. One might let me
into his mother's tavern or childhood
farmhouse in the old country. Another
to a diary describing the scorching
desert her parents crossed
to this land of maples and pines.

A few keys kept safe her treasures
not worth a dime: plastic purses, ring
with a blue glass stone, christening flowers
once pinned to the white dress
her brother wore forty-two years before
he burned black beneath a Pontiac
set aflame by the drunk who hit him
in a perfect perpendicular,
letters written in her husband's mother
tongue that no one left here can speak.

Skeleton key for the cedar closet
opens to three generations
of handmade dresses, skirts, suits
tight in their plastic sheathes
and at the very back, her tiny
wedding dress, pearls tinted gray
like her hair on the pillow
the night I couldn't find the key
to her breath. I remember
the strands as silver streaks
across a white sky, keys to a door
none of the living can enter.

Remodeling

Those are your toe kicks—
the place where you slam
the snow off your big work boot.
You may want to dance
in the hallway to your window jam,
which is sticking. Don't worry
about the ceiling crumbling
down on your headache.
We got you with our box cribs.
Yeah, it's your crib, but it's our box
while we're tearing through
your walls. Remember, it's all
about the studs, the I-beam,
and reinforcements if you know
what I mean. We will damp-proof
every inch of your basement.
Don't worry, that's only a trickle
of water. No need to be alarmed.
Why would you think the monster
clog in your stationary tub
has anything to do with the dry wall
you think you see stuffed
down the drain? We would never.
We know we got to get it right,
or you'll rubblize us,
hang us from the rafters.

Close the Door, Don't Touch That

even though it's nothing but a mess—
jars and coffee cans
of screws, nails, bolts, nuts,
o-rings, spools of wire in six different gauges,
pliers, flatheads, wire-cutters, Phillips.
How many hammers, wrenches? How many
light sockets, electrical housing
years out of code? Handsaws dangle
from pipes. Bits of chain and twine loop,
crawl like leafy vines. A table saw blocks
our path to the back of this pantry-thin,
basement room where the vice's jaws bite
a slice of twisted metal. All dust and clutter,
all manner of making or fixing out
on the workbench waiting for us
to wind it alive like a music box,
like an old phonograph with its trumpet-flower mouth.
A drill lies on the counter expecting uncle's hand.
And I'm in a highchair—all eyes,
dazzled and reaching for every-
thing that sparkled,
everything that could do something
I had yet to imagine.

The Red Fox Who Toys with the Dead

Carrying a sunset on his back,
the funeral home fox circles
an empty hearse where the dead pause
between rides. Perched atop
its shiny black hood, they pour
over maps of Mictlán, Valhalla,
Elysium, Bardo. Some toss dice, take bets.

I watch from the kitchen window
wondering who among them might play
Fox's game, chase the ball of fire he flips
off his tail into the arms of our old ash.
One specter so mourns her lost light,
she scales the tree's icy trunk, stretching
to rescue the dying day. A branch cracks,
falls through the windless sky catching
a glint from the moon's sickle. In a blink,
la muertita abandons Fox's red globe,
grasping for brighter beams.

Fox snarls, barks, nips at her toes,
finally turns to other shadows
until he corners one strong enough to pass
through cellar doors, slim enough to slip
between hairline cracks in the brick.
Beneath our basement stairs cluttered
with wrenches and rusty hinges, crowbars
and paint cans, the wraith finds a rope
for Fox to whirl to the ash's crown,
snag the girl, bring her and his ball back
down to earth where all belong.

I hear their clinks, their clanks,
the rope dragging itself across the walk.
But *la muertita* has long sailed beyond
its reach, beyond the dimmest stars,
galaxies farther than the red fox's radiance
heaped in a crow's nest ablaze with black
cackles. Gray as a grandfather, he drops
his ears, tail; watches the hearse slink
away; retreats in his own tracks
slowly filling with snow.

Good Boots

(for Roberto)

It required good boots—
water-proofed, laced, and zipped,
fur at the ankle, waffle sole—
to walk three miles in three feet
of snow. All the way to the lake
without slush between toes.

Because I could keep moving,
see my breath, because hand-knit
woolen caps act like good boots,
I still hold your wolf's eyebrows,
clear lake eyes in my snapshot
of love. In snow to my knees,

I knew I could winter with you.

Tranquilo

Pumpkins summersault
across lawns lit by fireflies.
Scintillating music crickets
vertiginous missives
for sunflowers who spill
sleepy heads to seed.
Tranquilo, mi cariño,
I hear your griot heart cleaving
to the moon.
Your hymn will be singed hibiscus
en la madrugada.
History will empty its silences
from stoneware that pours
a dune of dust at your feet,
cascades grapes, ginger melons, cassia tea.
Feast.
Someday, we will all swim
into paleolithic pixels anyway. Let go
the cruciferous grime, and paint
with me this elusive magenta morning.

Unruly Urban Youth

When we slept in the back
bedroom of the ash-gray upper—
little raincloud tucked
in a city park between cattails
at the duck pond's northern curve
and the locked-down, fenced-in
tenement we called a high school—
I woke each morning at 6:00 a.m.
to the squawks and screaks
of baby robins hanging
by Christmas tinsel and twigs,
helicopter seeds and shredded
test scores, leaves, love notes
patch-worked and tree-sapped
to the metal awning that pinged
when pecked, screeched like a chalk-
board against talons. Such ruckus,
such shrill panic in hunger's
unruly demands for nurture
or escape, such riotous music
thundering my eyes open
just in time to watch two tiny deer
appear in the bushes of your hair,
both decked out in their full regalia—
their clattering racks of antlers.

Because Home Is You

(for Roberto)

When I no longer must push your chair
in, pick up broken shards of water
glasses and my favorite clay pot,
dash for foaming soap that will lift
soup stains from the tablecloth where you sit.
When two in the morning no longer means
stealing my pillow back, wrestling blankets
from beneath your flesh furnace,
warming my shiver there. When our kitchen
counter is freed of pill bottles, extra milk
no longer curdles or freezes at the back
of the fridge, extra jars of curry stop
falling from the crowded cupboards—
worry for our cash-poor tomorrow.
When no dissonant timbre rises
through floor vents from a basement
bursting with music, books, and nothing
calls me to my third-generation rocker
near the window to watch dogs fetch
beneath guardian trees, will I buckle
at the silent threshold, cross the street,
and dive into pools of poplar leaves,
or strike a match and burn it all down?

Bookman

(after *Roger,* Marc Perlish's photograph of Bookman's Alley
and owner Roger Carlson)

"Yet he abandoned all to make a book and a labyrinth . . . No one
realized that the book and the labyrinth were one and the same."
—Jorge Luis Borges, from "The Garden of Forking Paths"

My years spent wandering cochlear
        paths around mounds of gold leaf,
                torqued paperback towers, shelves
groaning when I brace my weight, tug
        at a volume slim as its Preface Thin font.

        Spelunking aisles so narrow
barely a shadow could pass, I've found myself
        lost in a knot of voices
                wrestling for my ear, din
        unraveling me until I've crawled
back to silent letters a f l o a t
        in white fields. Ghosts
                never shut their traps
until you pay them some attention.

Today I hunker down with a friend
        in this den. We work late
                divesting me of *Country,*
Bix Beiderbecke, *Saskatchewan Trees.*

I'll consume my last hours in the aven
        of this cave tucked
                behind stalagmites of type, hunched
over ruins, sleeves rolled up and ready
        to turn infinite pages.
Everything is there: the minute history
        of the future . . . the interpolations
of every book in all books.

How to decipher the morphology of dream,
the moonmilk of words?
There is no key, and *obviously,*
no one expects to discover anything.
But look, I've left you a broom to sweep away
fallen commas, stray *k*'s and *j*'s dangling
from cobwebs, the frayed receipts
and torn corners that have marked
my ellipses into unmapped fissures,
subterranean canyons. Look,
this trail of breadcrumbs for you.

IV

"In a dream within a dream, I dreamt a dream"
—Lawrence Ferlinghetti, from "Rough Song of Animals Dying"

"now it is done,
and i feel just like
the grandmothers who,
after the hussy has gone,
sit holding her photograph
and sighing, *wasn't she*
beautiful? wasn't she beautiful?"
—Lucille Clifton, from "to my last period"

Middle Age Dreams

So that old lover, the one I didn't remember
when I ran into him at a bookfair
ten years after we ate strawberries
off each other's skin in a steamy tent
erected on the sandy bank of a river,
the one who approached me all smiles
as if we had eaten those strawberries
yesterday while I cast blank eyes
because I thought he might be
the long-lost friend I had dropped
acid with, in a house where fish swam
around fork and spoon, dipped in
and out of a coffee cup because,
you know, all aquariums are tables
set for breakfast. Not that one, but
the one who left me driveling
in puddles while he drifted across country
to join a Buddhist monastery. Yes,
that old lover shows up at 4:00 a.m.
I've already married him twice,
the second wedding only months before,
and now he's leaving me again.
I'm standing in a puddle that floods
the valley, no, the truck route (screw all this
pastoral shit and admit it, you live
on a truck route), about to marry a man
I've never seen in my life, nor whose fruit
I'd ever want to lick. When I try to shake out
the cobwebs and dry my feet on fresh sheets,
I tell husband about it, but all he can say is
"Where was I? You mean I wasn't even
present on our truck route?" And the dog
purr-growls which means she must go out.

Subtraction and Addition

A night minus husband = deep sleep
where you dream about husband
doing things he would never do—
leave you in a corner, so he can party
with celebrities on a barge out to sea.

Meanwhile, you've accumulated
a third brother who is aware
of your (and his) departed sibling
but won't utter aloud
that family minus brother = hole
in the bottom of the ship. He laughs

when you ask him to paddle you
to husband who holds
a glass of bourbon up to the moon
and howls while spinning
like Michael Jackson—
something husband would never do.

You minus words = empty space = panic:
stuck screen, gunked vocal cords.
Yes, a woman can shoot blanks, turn
into a red balloon that loudly
farts its way into a thicket of shame.

Why you, mute bubble? You've always been smitten
with the mutable—clownfish, chameleon,
seahorse, selkie, (ice cube).
You should be the trumpeter
that calls them all home.

Chivalry

When husband narrates his youthful escapades
tracing a figure eight in his jalopy around
the United States, living with hash farmers
in Morocco, and hitchhiking the coast of Spain,
he must also tell me about how his first Brenda
tied her sheets, pillowcases, and blouses together
and tossed them out the sixth-story window
like a rope. How he climbed them all the way up
to do the nasty with Brenda Rapunzel who had lost
her golden braid in a round of Spin the Bottle.
His gallant ascent for her pomegranate lips,
apricot eyes, and fresh berries is hotter than anything
I can provoke by flashing my fleece pajamas
and fuzzy bunny slippers past the front door
while he's shoveling snow. *Oh youth,* I sigh

as I fall asleep on a flannel-covered pillow,
drift off to a land where the corseted little queen
who stole my name reclines on a gold divan
with her plush obligations and smite scroll,
as she parlances unfinished business with the brigade
of knighted suitors outside her window. They play
no lutes, no mandolins, no flutes, no violins.
Wear no swashbuckling ruffled shirts open
to their six-packs and climb no nightdresses
to Brenda's tresses. Instead, they flaunt dirty
fingernails, bad breath, and lewd chewing. Spit
slang, smacking and smooching her filched name,
as they demand pregnancy into perpetuity
and every single one of their chivalrous sons.

Peep Show

A fat finger called menopause hit the pause
button on my sex dreams. But here and there,
the mind still arm-wrestles for a peep show.
After a drought, husband's tongue is all
meerkat and will-o'-the-wisp. I'm at the edge
of my madwoman's river, ready to dive
when, without warning, husband rises,
steps into a hot air balloon, cuts the ropes.
I'm pleading for the rest of the preamble,
for a piano run to the hot riff's summit,
so I can stretch my neck around,
part pink katydid, part praying mantis,
but he's as far away as the horizon now,
caught in his own dream.

Endless assemblage,

the house grows open
entries to
        sunken dens, living
rooms that watch. Try not to look
        in back behind. You
swish past hairless tails
        rustling in the walls,
Cortázar's green velvet armchair
        always empty inside
        the inside of a stranger
until stairs tumble
        to a formal dining room
        where you are served
your own tongue. Dangling
        teacups wag toward a door.

You lift blankets clinging to god-
mother's bones. If you fill her
chest with tears, they'll swim
through the slats of her ribs,
spill a river at your feet. No

matter, in a month, the kitchens
will multiply. You'll back in-
        to a black-and-white one. Here
a mother feeds five gathered
'round a gray Formica table, one
        in a highchair screaming,
a bowl of cereal upside
        down on his head, milk drip-
        ping off his nose, chin.
She stands in the puddle, apologizes
        for occupying. The house

was empty, she says, and in this room,
        daylight. She promises
to pack, leave before you can open
        any more doors, your mouth. You have
grown a new tongue. Tell her
        to stay. There are three more
kitchens up the hall, one stocked
with green peppers and ice.

Question the benevolence

in the sliver of shelter you've offered,
relieved, as you are, to drop in-
to this nostalgia with its '59
Westinghouse still warm
to the touch. You clutch
the table's chrome edges, safe
and tucked away from what hovers
above the tiny hairs
at the back of your neck.
Where will you turn
if it ever lets you loose?

You'll say to find the only door out.
You'll say to greater acts of kindness.
You'll say toward the southern coast
of a country across the sea where
the one you love still wanders.

Then you'll take steps
to escape your cell,
steps so tiny
that 32 million wall to wall
will carry you from Barcelona
to Algeciras. There a boatman waits
for you to cross the bay. He snags
his anchor on a skeleton
of coral, drops
his head in a dream
of rusty hinges and brigs
that he begs not to enter.
But as you draw near, you hear
the clang of his cup
against the bars, the moans
beneath his dog-tired feet.

Going under

is the safest risk you can take.
Anesthesia plunge into black holes
where no one can touch you while
they are all touching you. The anxiety
of daylight floods through cracked windows,
but you float in a cool blur—school of fish
swimming past your empty wallet,
hard deadlines, chronic cough that keeps
you awake all night. Starfish blink
in the grout between tiles, and you wonder
if the ocean is really just a public pool,
your swim shorts plunging to your ankles
when a fake tidal wave sucks you down
and spits you out, butt like a baby's
bare to the world. You think you hear
the crowd clapping as you await the slap
into breath, your new life, but your eyelids,
glued shut, struggle to pull apart
for the nurse trying to whisper you
back. How short the time they left you
alone while four of them crowded
around you. To go back under might be
the safest risk you could take.

Shipping and Receiving

Sick of fumbling with lunch sack, purse,
umbrella, mask, keys, and the two-ton
backpack overflowing with unread essays,
laptop discussion posts, poems caught
in the jammed zipper, I slam it all down
on the kitchen table and declare to the dog
that "I quit!" I will never again work
anywhere that sends me home to work
even harder all weekend long. End of story,
period, punto, ya! I decide to shift

careers, go into shipping and receiving
when I find my feet in thick-soled boots
on a cement floor, pencil behind my ear,
clipboard in hand, colossal rolls of packing
tape and boxes large as coffins, small as keys.
When I raise my hand above my head,
semi-trucks turn on their engines, roll
into formation. My clipboard clamps
one end of a scroll that drops past my feet,
trails me around the warehouse like a tail.
And so I ship . . .

every essay current and future students
will write, paper clips caught in their corners,
to a grading factory in Antarctica
where workers are hungry for words.

my email and all social media accounts
with their humblebragging
to the ether from whence they came.

parking tickets, alarm clocks, blue light,
and dry eye, long lines and loud
commercials to the Island of Irritation.

foothills of snow at every crosswalk
to Tampa, Dallas, and Orange County
specially packaged with a dozen stalactite
icicles to hang from their metal awnings.

light pollution to the darkest corners
of hell, air pollution back to the factories
that produced it, estimated arrival well
after third shift has bussed home.

Our mothers' arthritic knees, swollen
ankles, and bulging disks on shooting
stars to Pluto where pain's roots
shrivel in the dark, never to bud.

I send cancer to its crabby constellation
where cells heal in each other's light.
Politicians to the world's largest library
where books finally shut their fat mouths.

Macroaggressions, microaggressions,
all our isms I zap back
two million years so we can choose
to evolve without them.

Stop-and-frisk, billy clubs, chokeholds,
bullet holes, knees on necks to a police
state that lives only in our history books.

Hunger to pastures turned gardens,
row upon row of corn, beans, squash,
carrots, potatoes, onions, tomatoes,
lettuce. Let there be lettuce.

Special delivery: the right wing to Alcatraz
where they must read and recite critical
race theory while bowing to unions
who've rescued them from twelve-hour shifts.

All pandemics and their anti-vaxxers
on an Elon Musk spaceship to a distant
zombie galaxy about to be devoured
by its starved cannibal neighbor.

The itch I cannot reach to breeding
mosquitos so they can tear open
red bumps in the middles of their own backs.

I consider shipping the mosquitos as well,
but then remember dragonflies, bats, birds,
fish, frogs, turtles and, instead, order
a crate of calamine lotion. This I will receive

along with a black-and-white dog named Maya
and the human I love who walks her in healthy
forests awash with birds, bear, fox, deer,
berries, moss, and mushroom spores.

A comfortable bed, books, blankets for all,
students who whisper their poems in my ears,
a cup of cinnamon tea, a mug of Belgian beer.

Butternut squash, sage, basil, ajo,
clove, canela, cominos, tamales,
tomate, sopa de tortilla, sopa de papa,
many pachangas, muchos mariachis.

Every instrument and its music,
tiny sculptures blown together by wind,
fresh water, endangered languages
and species in multiple shipments.

All those killed for their color, their culture,
religion, poverty, for the one they love.
The eighty-one women murdered by men
in twenty-eight days—all of them alive again

con mis tias y tios, abuelos y primos,
mi papá y hermanito. A flatbed full
of cempazuchitl to light their way.
Visits from ancestors. Visits from stars.

Mirrors

My mother makes tea
in the cabin's orange kitchen,
limping on arthritic knees
as my right knee gives out
when I rise to help her.

In her hands wrapped around
a lime-green cup, I see my own
long fingers, once thin, now
thickening around the wedding band
I can no longer pull off,
circle engraved with the Hopi symbol
for marriage—waves of water always
in motion, always lapping home.

Today, she gifts me
black-and-white photographs
of her mother as a pudgy baby,
her parents' roaring twenties wedding,
and her four-year-old self sitting
in an outhouse, bib overalls
in a puddle around her ankles.

I haven't told her about the night
I flashed past a candlelit mirror,
glanced up, and peered
into my great-grandmother's face,
webs of purple veins, gray strands
at her temples, and ninety-eight years
of worry wrinkled around her black eyes
that stared straight through mine.

Vexed

I'm so fat with stress that I can't fit
under the umbrella. When it rains,
my incredible hulk squeaks, soaked,
but mammoth breasts keep my feet dry.
Drops rolling off my back flood
the garden, drowning all my flowers.

Pink cheeks are overblown balloons
about to pop. In red, I am a forest fire,
razing all the tiny towns at my hem.
In turquoise, the Caribbean Sea stretching
from Colombia to Cuba, Mexico to Venezuela.
I will wash away continents with one swish
of my sea-foam scarf. When I wear brown,
Sequoia forest, mighty river of clay.

But most days, the taut whip keeps
me plodding—ox with nose yoked
to the mud, lumbering down the rows.
I sleep standing up, pushing hooved
dents in the floor of my stall.
Even in dreams, I pull the plow.

Notes

The Vicuña epigraph on page 6 is from Vicuña, Ceclia. *About to Happen.* Contemporary Arts Center, New Orleans and Siglio, 2017, p. 18.

The Monod epigraph on page 6 is from Monod, Jacques. *Chance and Necessity: An Essay on the Natural Philosophy of Modern Biology,* translated by Austryn Wainhouse. Vintage Books, 1972, p. 160.

"Nexus": The epigraph by Ana Mendieta is from *Women Artists of Color: A Bio-Critical Sourcebook,* edited by Phoebe Farris, Greenwood Press, 1999, p. 180. You may view photographs of Ana Mendieta's *Silueta* series in Olga Viso's *Unseen Mendieta: The Unpublished Works of Ana Mendieta,* Prestel Pub, 2008; Beatrice Merz's *Ana Mendieta: She Got Love,* Bilingual edition, 2014; and in other catalogues of the artist's work. A few from the series may be found online at *Museé: Vanguard of Photography Culture,* "Current Feature: Ana Mendieta": https://museemagazine.com/features/2017/11/20/w413qtz3xpqjl0lc2yzm1aar303951.

"Cien nombres para la muerte: Las jodidas/The Screwed Ones": You may view Erik Ricardo de Luna Genel's drawings *La Jodida, Las Huesos,* and *La Cargona* respectively online at *Lotería Collection,* "Lotería de los 100 Nombres":
http://loteria.elsewhere.org/100nombres/100Nombres-40.jpg.php.
http://loteria.elsewhere.org/100nombres/100Nombres-22.jpg.php.
http://loteria.elsewhere.org/100nombres/100Nombres-07.jpg.php.

"Cien nombres para la muerte: La hilacha/The Loose Thread": In Mayan cosmology, Ix Chel is the Goddess of the Moon, Water, Weaving, and Childbirth who set the world in motion. In her dark aspects, she is depicted as a crone wearing a skirt with crossed bones and carrying a serpent and jug of water. From it, she would pour rainstorms and floods onto the land to destroy, cleanse, and prepare for rebirth. You may view Erik Ricardo de Luna Genel's drawing *La Hilacha* online at *Lotería Collection,* "Lotería de los 100 Nombres": http://loteria.elsewhere.org/100nombres/100Nombres-25.jpg.php.

"Our Lady of Sorrows": You may view Ana Mendieta's *Untitled* from the *Silueta* series, which inspired this poem, online at the *Smithsonian American Art Museum*: https://americanart.si.edu/artwork/untitled-silueta-series-34658.

"Cien nombres para la muerte: La zapatona/The Fleet-Footed Woman": You may view Erik Ricardo de Luna Genel's drawing *La Zapatona* online at *Lotería*

Collection, "Lotería de los 100 Nombres":
http://loteria.elsewhere.org/100nombres/100Nombres-41.jpg.php.

"In Veiled Voices": You may view Harvey K. Littleton's *Blue Conical Intersection with Ruby and Orange Ellipsoid*, a piece strikingly similar to the one that inspired this poem, online at *Blackbird Archive*, "Harvey Littleton" here: https://blackbird.vcu.edu/v12n1/gallery/littleton_h/legacy.shtml. Also, the photograph of Littleton's *Ruby Conical Intersection with Amber Sphere* demonstrates the layers and "ghosts" in the piece that inspired my poem, although the colors are different. You may view it online at *Corning Museum of Glass*:
https://www.cmog.org/artwork/ruby-conical-intersection-amber-sphere.

"Shadow Dancing with the Living and the Dead": You may view photographs and video of Roy Staab's 2016 *Shadow Dance* installation at Villa Terrace in Milwaukee, Wisconsin at the following web sites: *Urban Milwaukee*, "The Old Man and the Reeds," https://urbanmilwaukee.com/2016/06/09/art-the-old-man-and-the-reeds/; *American Craft Council*, "Honoring Nature and Imperfection,"
https://www.craftcouncil.org/post/honoring-nature-and-imperfection; and YouTube, "Descending the Stairs to Shadow Dance," https://www.youtube.com/watch?v=_1PiapSFTHI.

"Chiral Formation": You may view photographs and video of Roy Staab's 2012 *Chiral Formation* installation on Little Lake, Lynden Sculpture Garden, Milwaukee, Wisconsin at the following web sites: *Roy Staab*, "Chiral Formation @ the Lynden Sculpture Garden Finished,"
http://roystaab.blogspot.com/2013/03/chiral-formation-lynden-sculpture.html
and *Vimeo*, "Chiral Formation at the Lynden Sculpture Garden," https://vimeo.com/48461994.

"Yegua's Daughter": You may view photographs of Ana Mendieta's triptych *On Giving Life*, 1975, in Olga Viso's *Unseen Mendieta: The Unpublished Works of Ana Mendieta*, Prestel Pub, 2008 and online at *Daros*, "Ana Mendita," https://www.daros-latinamerica.net/artwork/giving-life or at *with reference to death*,
https://withreferencetodeath.philippocock.net/blog/mendieta-ana-on-giving-life-1975/.

"Inverse": You may view a photograph of Amy Cropper's *Inverse*, painted ash and hawthorn, 2011, Lynden Sculpture Garden, Milwaukee, Wisconsin online at *Lynden Sculpture Garden*: https://www.lyndensculpturegarden.org/collection/inverse.

You may view Ana Mendieta's *Body Tracks*, paintings, 1982, in Beatrice Merz's *Ana Mendieta: She Got Love*, Bilingual edition, 2014; in Olga Viso's *Unseen*

Mendieta: The Unpublished Works of Ana Mendieta, Prestel Pub, 2008; and online at the following web sites: *Ana Mendieta blog*, https://anamendietaartist.tumblr.com/post/155431613063/ana-mendieta-body-tracks-1982; *Elephant*, "Image of the Day," https://elephant.art/iotd/ana-mendieta-untitled-body-tracks-1974/; and Franklin Furnace, "Performance and Politics," https://franklinfurnace.hemi.press/chapter/ana-mendieta/ana_mendieta_catalog/.

The Griffin epigraph on page 28 is from Griffin, Susan. *A Chorus of Stones: The Private Life of War*. Anchor, 1993.

"Because We Come from Everything" is a collage poem titled with and using a line from Juan Felipe Herrera's poem "Borderbus" (*Notes on the Assemblage*, City Lights, 2015). With the exception of a few conjunctions and prepositions such as "and" and "from," which I added, all of the language in this poem is borrowed from works by Mexican American and Native American authors whose books were removed from Tucson Public School classrooms when the Tucson United School District banned the district's Mexican American Studies Program under the 2010 law HB 2281. In 2017, a federal judge declared this law unconstitutional and enacted with discriminatory intent. The poem's phrases and lines were originally written by Gloria Anzaldúa, Lorna Dee Cervantes, Sylvia Chacón, Sandra Cisneros, Culture Clash, Joy Harjo, Cherrí Moraga, Eulalia Pérez, Tomás Rivera, Diane Rodríguez, Luis J. Rodríguez, Caridad Svich, Luis Alberto Urrea, Gina Valdés, Evangelina Vigil-Piñón, Tino Villanueva, and Bernice Zamora. This poem is for them.

"Ars Resistencia": The art of El Anatsui, which inspired the beginning of this poem, may be viewed online at *Brooklyn Museum*, "Gravity and Grace: Monumental Works by El Anatsui": https://www.brooklynmuseum.org/exhibitions/el_anatsui. The poem also references a performance art piece created by the Border Arts Workshop during which the collective's artists, Guillermo Gomez Peña among them, set up a dinner table across the US/Mexico border. Every time a Mexican national had to "pass the salt" to a fellow diner on the U.S. side of the table, they had to cross the border "illegally."

"Placa/Roll Call": You may view Charles "Chaz" Bojórquez's painting *Placa/Roll Call* online at *Smithsonian American Art Museum*: https://americanart.si.edu/artwork/placarollcall-32848.

"Public Promise": You may view Julian Correa's *Mixed Media on Canvas, 2007* online at UWM Report: Faculty/Staff Newsletter, Vol. 28, No. 6, September 2007, p. 8: https://minds.wisconsin.edu/bitstream/handle/1793/29032/R_Sept07Final.pdf?sequence=1.

The Giménez Smith epigraph on page 41 is from Giménez Smith, Carmen. *Milk and Filth.* University of Arizona Press, 2013, p. 58.

"Rupture": You may view Remedios Varo's painting *Ruptura,* 1955, in Elizabeth Goldson Luis-Martin's and Liliana Valenzuela's *The Magic of Remedios Varo,* National Museum of Women in the Arts, 2000 and online at *Wiki,* "Ruptura (Remedios Varo)": https://wikioo.org/es/paintings.php?refarticle=8LT5ZY&titlepainting=rupture&artistname=Remedios%20Varo.

"Bookman" borrows language from Jorge Luis Borges' story "The Library of Babel" (Borges, Jorge Luis. *Ficciones,* Grove Press, 1994), and the poem's epigraph is from Borges' story "The Garden of Forking Paths," 1941, reprinted in *Ficciones.* You may view Marc Perlish's photograph *Roger* online at *Fine Art America*: https://fineartamerica.com/featured/roger-marc-perlish.html?product=poster.

The Ferlinghetti epigraph on page 65 is from Ferlinghetti, Lawrence. *Northwest Ecolog,* City Lights Books, 1978.

The Clifton epigraph on page 65 is from Clifton, Lucille. *The Collected Poems of Lucille Clifton, 1965–2010,* edited by Kevin Young and Michael S. Glaser, BOA Editions Ltd., 2012, p. 381.

Acknowledgments

Thanks to the following editors and publications where some of these poems or earlier versions of them first appeared.

Anthologies:
Brute Neighbors: Urban Nature Poetry, Prose & Photography; Cave Canem Anthology XIII: Poems 2010–2011; Celebrating Wisconsin People: 2019 Wisconsin Fellowship of Poets Calendar; City Creatures: Animal Encounters in Chicago's Urban Wilderness; Grabbed: Poets and Writers on Sexual Assault, Empowerment, and Healing; I Didn't Know There Were Latinos in Wisconsin; Kinship: Belonging in a World of Relations: Planet, vol. 1; *Return to the Gathering Place of the Waters: Milwaukee Poets in 2017; The Oxeye Reader; What Will I Find? Photographs, Music, and Poetry: An Homage.*

Journals:
Court Green, issue 16; *Cuadernos de ALDEEU,* no. 26; *Fifth Wednesday Journal,* issue 13; *Jet Fuel Review,* vol. 10, no. 3; *Pilgrimage,* vol. 35, no. 3; *Poetry,* vol. 207, no. 6; *TAB: The Journal of Poetry and Poetics,* vol. 10, no. 4; *Verse Wisconsin,* no. 109; *Verse Wisconsin,* no. 110; *Verse Wisconsin,* no. 113.

Other:
The Best American Poetry Blog—Because We Come from Everything: Poetry and Migration; *The Quarry: A Social Justice Poetry Database;* Woodland Pattern Book Center: "In Veiled Voices," broadside.

In conjunction with the Smithsonian American Art Museum's 2013 exhibit "Our America: The Latino Presence in American Art," Letras Latinas, the literary program of the University of Notre Dame's Institute for Latino Studies, launched Pintura: Palabra: A Project in Ekphrasis, a multi-year initiative to encourage the creation of art-inspired poetry. In 2014, fellow poet Valerie Martínez and I were invited to design and teach the inaugural master workshop for this initiative at the Smithsonian in Washington, DC, during which I wrote the initial drafts of "Our Lady of Sorrows" and "Placa/Roll Call." I am indebted to Letras Latinas director Francisco Aragón, exhibit curator E. Carmen Ramos, collaborator Valerie Martínez, and all of the workshop fellows for this delightful and educative experience which has inspired and influenced many ekphrastic poems in the years since.

Thank you to the University of Wisconsin-Milwaukee for the 2020–2021 sabbatical which afforded me the time to finish this collection.

A mis queridos tíos Elia y Karel por encender el fuego de la creatividad y por el gran regalo de nuestro hogar, mil gracias. Les extraño y les amaré todos los días de me vida.

To my husband, Roberto Harrison; my parents, José and Dee Cárdenas; the exquisitely talented poets in my writers' group, Nicole Callihan, Jane Creighton, Laura Cronk, Iris Dunkle, Catherine Esposito Prescott, Janet Jennerjohn, Michele Kotler, Ruth Ellen Kocher, Kristen Peterson Kaszubowski, Bethany Price, Robin Reagler, Suzanne Wise, and Marion Wrenn; and to those abiding friends who have kept the fire burning, Francisco Aragón, Reneé Cárdenas, Ching-In Chen, Carlos Cumpían, Gina Franco, Mauricio Kilwein Guevara, Valerie Martínez, Siwar Masannat, Urayoan Noel, Soham Patel, Ruben Quesada, Regine Rousseau, Jeanne Theoharis, Emma Trelles, and Aidé Rodríguez Zamudio—for your inspiration and encouragement, all the gratitude and love I can possibly muster!

Abrazotes to Woodland Pattern Literary Center—the heart of the arts and master community builder in the city I call home—to its founders, Anne Kingsbury and Karl Gartung, and its current dynamic duo, Directors Jenni Gropp and Laura Solomon. I can't imagine Milwaukee without you!

To my little brother Daniel, now off in other realms, I keep close your incredible grace, and I know you are rockin' somewhere. I can hear the electric guitars.

Biographical Note

Brenda Cárdenas is the author of *Boomerang* (Bilingual Press) and the chapbooks *Bread of the Earth/The Last Colors* with her husband Roberto Harrison; *Achiote Seeds/Semillas de Achiote* with Cristina García, Emmy Pérez, and Gabriela Erandi Rico; and *From the Tongues of Brick and Stone*. She also coedited *Resist Much/Obey Little: Inaugural Poems to the Resistance* (Spuyten Duyvil Press) and *Between the Heart and the Land: Latina Poets in the Midwest* (MARCH/Abrazo Press). Cárdenas has served as faculty for the CantoMundo writers' retreat and as Milwaukee Poet Laureate. She currently teaches Creative Writing and Latinx Literature at the University of Wisconsin-Milwaukee.